For Those Who Dream at Night

Mays Mango

For Those Who Dream at Night © 2022
Mays Mango

All rights reserved.

No part of this publication may be
reproduced, stored in a retrieval system, or
transmitted, in any form or by any means,
electronic, mechanical, photocopying,
recording or otherwise, without the prior
written permission of the presenters.

Mays Mango asserts the moral right to be
identified as author of this work.

Presentation by *BookLeaf Publishing*

Web: www.bookleafpub.com

E-mail: info@bookleafpub.com

ISBN: 9789357616010

First edition 2022

ACKNOWLEDGEMENT

I would like to praise Allah (God) who has granted me countless blessings, the knowledge, and the opportunity to write this book.

No amount of words could formulate the gratitude I have for my parents.

They encourage, support, and love me unconditionally.

Without them, I would have never experienced the magnitude of opportunities I have thus far.

I appreciate my respectable teacher, Aicha Toure, for inspiring me to write this book. I thank her for being patient, advising, and guiding me throughout this experience.

Also, I want to thank everyone who encouraged me to write this book in any way.

Your continuous support and prayers are much appreciated.

Cursed Touch

Beware of the cursed mountains
They would say
Though there live healers, just one look in their
eyes
Your family will decay
...
Day after day,
Boredom and loneliness faced her
Locked up in a castle
She wept to be free
A sad, lonely princess was she.
Anything she touched would die.
Turn gray and black
Standing at the edge
It seemed so farfetched
She saw the rest of the world
Far larger than her dream world
A city full of people.
Beyond that,
she could see the Mountain of curses
The girl was cursed, neglected, never respected
She had enough of hiding,
of lurking in shadows
People looking down on her
Never smiled

not a reason to
Always walked with her head down
She feels isolated
tired of being left out,
tired of being in doubt
She's not a shadow
but a person with feelings
She has heard of the myths
But anything is better than this

Cursed Illusions

The girl snuck out late
swiftly snuck to the right
Ending in the dead forest
She came across a captivating sight
She couldn't help but enter
"The flowers will give you attention,"
"The breeze will give you direction"
She heard a voice say as she walked
"Fine green leaves
Rich brown soil
In here
you hope to stay forever "
She heard it say
"Don't need to worry
Right here, a safe place indeed"
It said
"In this world
Our garden, our place
Where we are both out of place."

Cursed End

Then it hit her
She was being lured in!
Suddenly! she was back in the dead forest!
There was a powerful presence in the air
Fear overwhelmed her
Chuckles filled her in a blur
Footsteps echoed, inching closer
Terror exploded in her
She bolted to her feet
Running at highest speed
The forest being too dark
She didn't know where to park
She wanted to hide
But she knew wherever she went
it would tend
"What are you doing here?"
"Are you asking for a death wish?"
"Leave before you parish"
A deep eerie voice said
She bolted deeper into the forest
With no rest
Her breath came quick
She hid behind trees
The breeze made her freeze
She felt it coming closer

The girl took her gloves off
 ready to kill
"Didn't I tell you to leave?"
The voice sounded irritated
"Since you want to stay
don't blame me if you decay"
The voice disappeared
Leaving her behind
As she was running,
throbbing bruises on her feet
And Scrapes all over her knees
Her brain went a mile per hour
She had to figure out a way to gain power
Suddenly she heard the voice
But instead
It was in her head
It was the same deep, dark voice that she heard
"Surprise"
The girl's breathing sped
Her heart galloped
Wearing a frown
She looked to see if it was around
"No use, I'm in your head"
 She chose her words wisely
"I feel sickly"
"I am to be healed"
She said
"Have you not heard of the myths you fool, "
It amusingly said

"For you will not leave unscathed"
"You have two options"
It said
" If you heal, you stay.
 Or die in vain and decay"

Hallucinations

The forbidden forest
Where creatures are promised.
Do not look in the eye.
For if you do
Expect your goodbyes
And be careful
 never defy
…
 In nature,
she would oversee
A beautiful path
Beauties that run wild and free
Leaves like feathers forfeit
Creating a stunning red carpet
 Many hues of red she sees
From the brightest
To the dullest.
Trees sway to silent tunes
As if it were afternoon
Suddenly, dreadfulness consumed the air
As she steps further
She tries to make out
Once breathtaking beauty,
 now an awful lookout
Everything died out

She tried to turn back
Yet something pulled at her
The beautiful vibrant colors
Now dull and dark
Leaned tree barks
Now black and leafless

Hallucinations

She stopped in her tracks and looked back
Suddenly attacked…
she did not know for exact
It was invisible
 finally got away
Each passing second
The sky darkens
Something crawled up her leg
Not an insect
But a hand
She remembered the myths
And kept her eyes shut
Suddenly! She is pushed into a firm tree
blood spilled out her mouth everywhere
She gazed all around
Out of nowhere
 Billions and trillions of tiny black spiders
surround her
She could not take it
She shut her eyes
 Surrendering to the torments of the
Forbidden forest.

The Mystery Man

They warned us about the Mystery man
Always a deep secret in his plan
 He was difficult to understand
Since he began
No wonder he was called the Mystery man
…
I checked my watch
It was already 3:00 A.M.
What am I still doing out here?
I question myself
I heard footsteps
I asked
"Is anybody there?"
The streetlights flickered on and off in a ghastly
way
I looked back
I saw a black figure
It took off before I could make out what it was
I hear my heart pounding in my ears
I took in my surrounding
I am near the bus stop
I start walking toward it
I suddenly stop
the black figure from before
Sitting not too far

His skin ashed
His head had not a single hair
Two big, black eyes stared at me
Goosebumps form his creepy grin
Suddenly walking towards me
I dashed out
I needed to be anywhere else
away from that man
I could not stop the urge to look back
the man disappeared
No wonder
 he was called the Mystery man
I turn to go home
Suddenly! I halt
The Mystery man,
He towered over me.
 My first instinct was to – AHH!

The Mystery Man

I woke up panting,
covered in sweat
My hair plastered to my forehead and neck
I tossed my blanket off my sweating body
I was out of breath,
My heart was beating too fast
It took a moment to feel normal again
 Phew, it's just a dream.
I thought as I go wash my face
The water was cold and fresh
I look in the mirror
 Something was behind me
A tall black figure
It was the Mystery man.

Inspired by Malak Alabsi

Alone at night

She stares into endless space
Something pulls her back
She turns around
To see reflections of her face
Written on the shiny mirror
In blood-red was a single word
"Die"
Suddenly! A loud slam!
Bathroom door closed!
Lights went out!
Leaving her in total darkness!
She tries opening the door
To no avail! She was trapped!
She felt a hand choking her
To the touch the hands
felt like nothing
 eerie giggles fills her ears
She closed her eyes and screamed
Hard enough to shred her throat
She opened her eyes to find nothing
She tried opening the door again
It was unlocked
She ran up to her room as if being chased
There, horror filling her eyes
Her clothes tossed everywhere

Her books lying on the ground
The sheets and pillows crumpled on the floor
The most gruesome of all
written on her wall
in blood
"You cannot hide from fate"
She bolted out her room into her front yard at
full speed
"Run if you want. I'll always catch you"
She heard it echo

Raging Vengence

Vengeance is all I want
The burning pain of hatred.
The loathing in my heart
Blooming into a harsh pleasant revenge
It is all I long for
Constant rage rests deep in me
The thought
Oh, so bitterly sweet
I will tear you into fragments of my pain
Mentally damage your very thoughts
as you did to me
Vengeance is all I need
You made me live in misery
Oppressed me
Made me suffer
The reason I'm now broken!
Far gone.
It's my turn
Vengeance is all I crave
When the misfortune I lay upon you manifests
Never will you forget
You have committed a huge mistake.

Haunted Vengeance

Lights flicker in bed
Windows open
A gust of cold wind
Ran shivers up her spine
Something is hovering in thin air
Voices fill her ears
The Loser's face suddenly blocked her vision.
Frightened, she flees
Suddenly, pushed down steep stairs
Fracturing many bones
She tried to crawl out
Useless,
The ghost wouldn't let her
punching and kicking,
Her breaths came quickly
horrified of her own home
She took off to her mother's house
…
Finally dozing off
creaky sounds of stairs robbed her sleep
Her mother entered the room
Creepy grins
on her face
Her mother grabbed a knife
Coming at her in full speed

A brief pause,
her mother cuts herself
Staring right through the girl
As she harms herself
incapable of doing anything
She ran away
Wherever she ran
It would follow
"Leave me alone or…! "
The girl screamed in terror
"Or What?
What will you do?
 Kill me? I'm already dead"
"You tortured me,
made me suffer,
made my life a living hell"
"Watched me drift"
"I'll slowly take your life
Torturing you, haunting you, and making you
suffer"
"One life for another
My friend, you have made a huge mistake"

Nightmares

There are some awful kinds of dreams
Ones which I want to avoid,
Ones that cause all fear to rise
Ones when I close my eyes
Longing for sweet dreams to knock
All I get is nightmares' harsh bang
Tears stream down
Screaming loud enough to shred my dry throat
They wrap themselves around me at night
No matter what I do
They keep replaying
I just want to keep living my Dream
Instead of waking up to a bad Dream
These dark thoughts follow
Now they don't only darken my nights
 but also my precious days
They don't seem to leave me
And now, darkness continues to grow inside me
I still remember
And can't seem to forget
The nights I woke up intense
No hope for recovery
Because I have to face them on my own again
But they will never win
I'll escape the looming shadows
With dawn's first light

To be Alone...

I sink my doubts and worries
beneath this cold Earth
Hoping they would never come up
But in the depths of night
They creep up
Dragging me
 to the deepest corners of my mind
The Darkness
It calls me in
Shatters me in despair
The silence is deafening
Chaos rising
Lost in a world of endless fear
When dark comes
I do not fear
What I fear is being alone
 with my thoughts
And chaos inside
 When I lay my head down
And slowly drift away
That is when
 I get carried away

Lost

You never said farewell
You left before I knew it,
Many times I needed you,
Many times I cried.
In my heart, you held a place,
That no one could ever replace.
You were there from the very begging.
You helped me grow
It pained me to see you go
It tore my heart to lose you,
 you didn't go alone
part of me left with you,
Now I sit here by myself, thinking
All of this could end
That I could be with you again
I decided
 I couldn't take it anymore
I wanted to join you
I walk in front of a massive truck
I think of certain people, but they don't care
For the first time, I think of myself
But its too late
 now I'm lying on the street,
My blood, all around me,
I can hear the paramedic

"She won't make it."
Pain is overcoming me!
Yet, I know everything will be alright
Since I'll be with you
"Why cry for me?
I'm finally free
Don't forget me
Don't blame yourself
Don't do this to yourself
Laugh at all things we used to do
And not with your head so low
Be the flourishing grass above me
And if you weaken, just remember
For this trip, all must take
It's all part of the master plan"
The voice says before vanishing into thin air
I open my eyes
I can breathe again
Pain still everywhere
yet it was bearable
My head, no longer fuzzy
The voice told me to stay
And think of the better days
To breathe
To laugh
and remember those who love me
the pain will pass
To give myself kindness
And give myself care

The Mending Forest

Come back to the forest!
Where time goes slow and steady
to mend your worries
The voice shall say
Come back to the wild
To make friends with trees
and wander through streams
The voice shall say
Come back to nature
When you need somewhere to belong
I have been waiting for so long"
The voice shall say
Come back home
The forest is waiting for you

Wanted White

The cold fresh air of night
   calls her in
 as trees hum a familiar song
 She decides to surrender
to beautiful hums of the forest
 The girl wandered through dangerous beautiful
woodland
Where tall trees and pointy-leaved bushes
crowded close
She couldn't remember the last time she was
alone
At that moment something caught her attention
She spun to stare into the woods
She heard it
Someone is following her
  she was being lured in
She cursed herself for wandering without
protection
 the girl walked faster
  she looked back,
 to her great surprise
 A pair of shining red eyes staring back
 the girl ran for quite a while
She understood what Red eyes was doing
 Red eyes was trying to wear her out

The girl knew Red eyes could not be human
She had no choice but to give into
Her other side.
She turned into a beautifully menacing wolf
As white as snow
Her silence hearing all around
The silence before whatever or whoever
comes next
She would not look at the world
Her eyes stayed closed
In between deep breaths
She would open her eyes
The beauty would consume her
Suddenly,
Black consumes her vision
She hears something hovering beside her ear
Piercingly Wicked laughs fill her ears

The Strangest Dream

The Dream always turns into a Nightmare
In it, someone always after her
She is too afraid to fall asleep
Because they will start
and cause such a fright
 When she goes to sleep, she prays
 just to sleep tonight until day
 When she finally curled up in bed
she didn't think she would ever sleep
Yet she slept like the dead
her dreams felt strangely real
In her Dream
She left her apartment
Leaving the door wide open
She walked late at night through her
neighborhood
The night sky glowed where bright city lights
stood
The Moon,
a glowing whitish gray
surrounded by a gorgeous ray
her shadow evident in its bright light
The girl strolled over to a beach
That was always out of reach
The pavement hurt and splintered her bare feet

But didn't miss a beat
she felt mosquitoes land on her
Yet didn't slap them away
finally golden sand beneath her feet
The cold air felt sweet
She stood in front of crashing waves
The ocean waves lapped slowly at shore
Mix of indigo and royal blue
under the glowing Moon
sand felt mushy and soft
she let her feet slip into cold water
The gentle sounds of the waves
almost sounded like a lullaby.
The movement of waves soothe her withered
heart
While her mind and body slowly drifted apart
She took in a deep breath of fresh ocean air
It was so peaceful and calm
In the shadows lurking
a pair of two, green shining eyes burning
 right through her soul
She knew she was getting attacked
Since everything went black
She woke up to tall black figures dragging her
into once beautifully lit up blue waves
now deep, greenish black
the water, thick and muddy
She pushed down against the suffocating water
She tried bringing herself toward the surface

To no avail, She was drowning
Something powerful was pulling at her
Pulling her down
She couldn't fight it
She couldn't move
She had no control
she just sank to the bottom of the deep, black
ocean
She couldn't breathe
She was drowning
and couldn't do anything about it
 The Dream ended abruptly
When she woke up the next morning
she was asleep on the floor
Covered in mosquito bites
With splinters all over her feet
And her whole body
  drenched and covered in black, drippy mud.
When her roommate asked
Why the front door was wide open
She had no idea
She couldn't remember her dreams

Trees

They have lived among nature
close to the future
grown exotic flowers
fed birds that made nests
in daylight hours
Watching tiny plants
with a little nurturing
grow into stirring beauties
In summertime
They have seen many swim in glittering pools
And under their shades,
 they provide safety!
So keep them clean
Don't let them lean
Help them rise
And they will keep us alive

Spring Ahead

On a beautiful spring day,
The girl wept loud
while sitting down,
 making flower bands in a field of flowers
Her grandmother approached her
"My dear, why cry on such a beautiful day?"
"Witness the flowers bloom
the soothing sounds of birds will comfort you
chirping and singing so clear"
"My dear, why cry on a lovely Green Day?
When Earth is dressed of greenery and life
Filled with flowers
Rivers freed from ice
After so many months of White"
"My dear, I know dark is all you've known
 Spring is like stepping into light
Watch spring create a canvas
From the greenery of plants
to the blue skies and round yellow sun"
"My dear these times are imperative
to spend with loved ones
Sunlight and things ahead
 will give you a reason to smile
So my dear, always look ahead"

My Garden

There are secret gardens that only I find
They are deeply hidden in my mind
 Birds sing sweet tunes
Awakening the flowers
Watching the beauty shower over me
No hate, or debate
only people being nice
Peace is all you find
An unbelievable place it is.
Where the deaf can hear
And blind can see
It is such a relaxing place to unwind
I hope one day this world comes true
I hope it's close
so I can stop hiding in my mind
My garden is a special place
That is close to my heart
Which I hope I can share with the rest of the
world one day

Printed in the USA
CPSIA information can be obtained
at www.ICGtesting.com
LVHW082042270124
769808LV00014B/858